Nature

INTRODUCTION

The natural world around you is full of fascinating things to i-SPY. Earth, the planet on which we all live, was created some 4500 million years ago. Such a vast span of time is impossible to imagine – it is roughly equivalent to sixty million human lifetimes! Over the ages, the planet has evolved and changed. At first there was no breathable air as we know it; there were no plants or animals and no blue sky. Now, millions of years later, there is a complex web of life; plants and animals, weather and rock are all part of the same great pattern. And remember, you are part of nature too.

No single book could ever hope to include everything that you could spot but in i-SPY Nature, you will find all kinds of things to look for – from clouds to rainbows, rocks and fossils to ice-cut valleys, trees to flowering plants, insects to mammals. Go out and keep your eyes open. Look under stones (not forgetting to put them back) and up at the sky. And don't forget, if you have a garden there is a lot to see there too. But make sure you follow this simple rule: 'Take only photographs. Leave only footprints'.

Take care! There are poisonous plants and dangerous animals in the countryside. NEVER pick or eat any plant unless you are certain that it is good to eat and watch out for dangerous animals that have a venomous bite or sting. Remember, NEVER go out at night unless accompanied by a responsible adult.

How to use your i-SPY book

As you work through this book, you will notice that the subjects are arranged in groups which are related to the kinds of places where you are likely to find things. You need 1000 points to send off for your i-SPY certificate (see page 64) but that is not too difficult because there are masses of points in every book. Each entry has a star or circle and points value beside it. The stars represent harder to spot entries. As you make each i-SPY, write your score in the circle or star. For entries where there is a question, double your score if you can answer it. Answers are shown on page 63.

CUMULUS

Points: 5

These are the best known 'cotton wool' clouds which, when they are small and on their own in the sky, suggest that there is fair weather still to come.

Points: 10

CUMULONIMBUS

These deep clouds are associated with heavy rain and thunderstorms. They form at low levels in the sky, which is why they contain so much moisture, and are dark and flat at the base.

Points: 10

STRATOCUMULUS

These layered clouds often form as cumulus clouds spread out across the sky. They may build up in thick, dark bands but usually lead only to showers.

ALTOCUMULUS

Points: 10

Altocumulus clouds form at high levels in the atmosphere. These clouds indicate that the high atmosphere is damp and unstable.

Points: 5

NIMBOSTRATUS

Nimbostratus form a thick blanket of cloud that usually covers the whole sky, hiding the sun or moon. It produces continuous heavy rain or snow.

Points: 10

CIRRUS

The thin wispy streaks of cirrus clouds are made up of ice particles and as they thicken, this suggests the approach of warm air, which may also lead to rain within 24 hours.

RAINBOW

Points: 15

double with answer

Rainbows appear when rays of sunlight are bent and split by raindrops in the air. The white sunlight is split into seven colours. There is no 'pot of gold' at the end of a rainbow.

What are the seven colours of a rainbow?

Points: 15

RED SKY AT NIGHT

'Red sky at night, shepherds' delight!' This old saying is to some extent accurate: red suggests that there is good weather to come.

SNOWFLAKE

Points: 15

Everybody enjoys snow! It is beautiful to look at but can cause problems too. No two snowflakes are the same.

Points: 15

HAILSTONES

Hailstones are balls of ice that are formed high in the clouds. They are usually only a few millimetres in diameter, but can grow to 15cm (6 inches) and weigh 500g. In these cases take cover!

COMMON PIPISTRELLE

Points: 30   Top Spot!

This tiny bat roosts in cracks in buildings and trees. It feeds on small flying insects which it hunts for over woodland, farmland, and moorland.

DAUBENTON'S BAT

Top Spot! **Points: 30** double with answer

About a quarter of the world's mammals are bats. This bat can be seen in the evening skimming over water, chasing flies.

True or False – Bats will get caught in your hair?

Points: 10

MUTE SWAN

This is one of the birds that we all enjoy feeding at the pond but watch out, they can get aggressive when they have a brood of cygnets (young swans).

MAGPIE

Points: 5

A common member of the crow family, magpies are black and white with a long tail. Their nest is a large ball of twigs, often found in a roadside bush.

HOUSE SPARROW

Points: 10

These cheeky sparrows are often seen dust bathing in flower beds or at the side of the road. They will happily eat crumbs and seeds from a bird table or feeder.

Points: 10

STARLING

In spring, if you hear a noise in your attic, it's likely to be a nest of starlings. They have been known to mimic sounds from their surroundings.

BLUE TIT

Points: 5

Their acrobatics on bird feeders fill us with admiration and these colourful birds are also the gardener's friend, as they eat lots of insect pests.

Points: 5

BLACKBIRD

The male blackbird in spring is truly handsome with his shiny black plumage and yellow beak. His melodious song signifies that winter is over at last.

MALLARD

Points: 5

The mallard is our most abundant wild duck and is a familiar bird to most people.

Points: 10

CANADA GEESE

Introduced into Europe more than 200 years ago, they are now native and can be seen in large flocks on lakes, park ponds or in the fields cropping grass.

ROBIN

Points: 5

Both male and female robin have the red breast and are almost impossible to tell apart. It doesn't matter, we love them both.

Points: 10

Hazel has been coppiced for centuries. The resulting poles provide firewood, hurdles and thatching spars. The familiar nuts are eaten by a wide variety of creatures, including us.

APPLE

Points: 10

All modern-day apple trees are descended from the wild crab apple. Domestic apple trees usually need a companion tree to pollinate them and then they can bear edible fruit.

PEAR

Points: 15

Pear trees grow up to 17m (56ft) in height and are thought to have originated in China where they have been grown for at least 3000 years. Pear wood is often used in the manufacture of musical instruments.

Points: 10

CHERRY

The cultivation of cherries died out in the UK during the Middle Ages but luckily, this healthy fruit was re-introduced by Henry VIII. Look for the pink flowers in May.

Points: 10

A deciduous member of the maple family that can grow to 35m (115ft) tall. Its most notable feature, however, is the keyed seeds, which are also known as 'helicopters' because of the way they spin as they fall from the tree.

COMMON YEW

Points: 15

This strong but springy wood was the best for making longbows. In more modern times it has been found that the leaves contain an effective anti-cancer treatment.

ENGLISH OAK

Points: 10

The oak is viewed as a symbol of strength and longevity. It is also very important to insects and other wildlife. Jays are responsible for planting more oak trees than humans!

COMMON HAWTHORN

Points: 10

Farmers appreciate this tree because it forms an impenetrable thorny hedge, ideal for containing animals in fields. Its bright red berries provide colour during autumn and winter.

Points: 10

HOLLY

To us the red berries on the holly mean one thing: Christmas! To wildlife, they can make the difference between surviving winter or not.

HORSE CHESTNUT

Points: 10

In spring the tree is covered with stunning white 'candles' and in the autumn there will be a crop of nuts which can be used to play conkers.

Points: 10

SILVER BIRCH

The silver birch is a beautiful tree that has long been associated with the start of new life, due to its outstanding ability to colonise newly-cleared land quickly.

LEYLAND CYPRUS

Points: 5

This tree is more commonly known as Leylandii and is often used in hedges. If not clipped it can reach heights of up to 30m (98ft).

Points: 10

This tree is covered in long, vicious 'black thorns'. It heralds the arrival of warmer weather by covering itself in white blossom. The fruit of the blackthorn is a small plum called a sloe.

ELDER

Points: 15

The elder is usually not much more than a bush. But it is versatile – it feeds birds and animals, the bark and flowers can make dyes and last but not least, a twig can make a good fishing float!

PRIMROSE

Points: 10

A true harbinger of spring. What could be nicer than driving down a country lane flanked by these beautiful pale yellow flowers?

Points: 5

COMMON DANDELION

The scourge of gardeners but beneficial to insects. The root of this plant has long been used by herbalists to stimulate the digestive system.

Points: 15

RED CAMPION

A tall plant that produces pink flowers on long stems in May and June. Bumble bees bite through the base of the plant to reach the store of nectar.

COMMON POPPY

Points: 10

This common plant appeared in their millions in the battlefields after World War I, and has been adopted as a symbol of peace and remembrance ever since.

RAGWORT

Points: 10

It is thought that steam trains helped to spread the seeds of this plant as they rushed by. Not good news for horses – ragwort is harmful if mixed with dried grasses and hay as feed.

Points: 15

COMMON GORSE

Gorse bushes flower in most months of the year. Their coconut-scented flowers are beneficial to honey bees and other pollinators. A delicious wine can be made from the yellow petals.

CREEPING BUTTERCUP

Points: 10

Its creeping habit will swamp all other plants and although pretty, it's actually poisonous and gloves should be worn when weeding.

Points: 15

YELLOW IRIS

The roots or rhizomes of this waterside plant used to be crushed and the resulting juice used to make a black dye or ink.

THRIFT

Points: 15

The name refers to its ability to flourish on rocky sea cliffs with very little fresh water or soil, all the while being subjected to wind and salt spray.

Points: 5

IVY

Ivy gives so much: late season nectar for butterflies; for birds it offers a place to build a nest, hide from predators and provides food from its berries.

SPEAR THISTLE

Points: 10

Since 1503, the thistle has been the symbol of Scotland. Its biennial habit makes it unpopular with gardeners but the large (40mm or 1.6 inch) flowers are much sought after by butterflies and bees.

Points: 10

DOG ROSE

The symbol of the British monarchy is a good source of vitamin C. The bright red hips can be made into rose hip syrup.

BRAMBLE

Points: 5

If you brave the straggly thorns, you will enjoy the pleasures of blackberrying! And the apple and blackberry pie that follows!

Points: 10

COMMON DUCKWEED

Duckweed is a strange but very valuable habitat – water-borne insects shelter beneath it and up above it's a staple diet of many water birds.

GROUND ELDER

Points: 5

The gardener's enemy brought here by the Romans as a herbal medicine; it's not going home any time soon so we might as well live with it and its pretty white flowers.

Points: 5

COMMON NETTLE

Apart from the obvious sting, this is a really versatile plant – it can be eaten, infused and provide relief from chest complaints.

Points: 30   Top Spot!

ADDER

Britain's only poisonous snake is shy and will glide silently away if at all possible. Seek urgent antivenom treatment from hospital if you're bitten by one!

GRASS SNAKE

Points: 25

Grass snakes may grow to 1m (3ft) in length. They live in grassy areas near rivers, ditches and streams and they are excellent swimmers. They do not have a venomous bite, but can still be scary!

Points: 20

STOAT

You can tell the playful and inquisitive stoat from the smaller weasel by the black tip it has at the end of its tail.

WEASEL

Points: 20

A small (up to 23cm or 9 inches excluding tail) but ferocious brown and white hunter. They need to eat a third of their own body weight every day.

Points: 30   **Top Spot!**

PINE MARTEN

They are becoming more common thanks to conservationists and have even been known to live in attics and feed at bird tables.

FERN

Points: 15

Ferns need rich, damp soil to thrive and this is why they love the woodland floor where they enjoy the shade.

Points: 10

LICHEN

The 17,000 species of lichens are not actually plants at all but a partnership between a fungus and algae. Some colonies may be 9000 years old.

Points: 25

AMMONITE

Anyone who has visited the beach at Lyme Regis in Dorset will be familiar with these fossils. The animals are extinct but they are related to modern squids and octopuses.

BELEMNITE

Points: 25

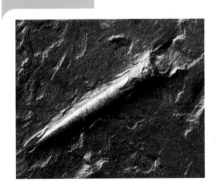

These fossils are also related to octopuses and squids but the bullet-shaped fossil is similar in many ways to the internal skeleton of a cuttlefish.

Points: 25

TRILOBITE

A trilobite is an arthropod – an animal with jointed legs like an insect or a spider. Fossils of this animal are found in rocks more than 400 million years old.

GRAPTOLITE

Top Spot!   **Points: 30**

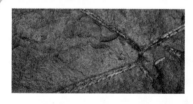

This fossil's name means 'stone writing' because when it was first discovered, this is what scientists thought the fossils looked like. This one is at least 400 million years old.

Points: 20

SEA URCHIN

Sea urchins are small, round spiny creatures that live on the sea floor. When they die their spines are rarely preserved, but their fragile shells often get washed up on the beach.

Points: 10

SANDY BEACH

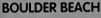

This kind of broad, gently sloping sandy beach occurs where the swell from the open sea rolls in, deposits some sand and pulls much of it back into the sea again.

BOULDER BEACH

Points: 15

When rocks are continuously washed to and fro in the water, the sharp edges are gradually worn away and they become rounded. This can take millions of years.

ROCKY SHORE

Points: 10

Where the rocks are below the high water mark, look out for rock pools where you might find crabs, shrimp, small fish or even a starfish.

 Points: 15

CLIFFS

The colour of the cliffs will depend on what kind of rock they are. White cliffs are made of chalk, which was formed from the skeletons of many billions of tiny animals which lived almost 100 million years ago.

WAVE-CUT PLATFORM

Points: 15

These are formed at the base of a cliff, sometimes by the erosive action of the waves, but landward erosion by freshwater is also sometimes the cause.

Points: 30   Top Spot!

SEA ARCH

A sea arch forms where the action of the waves hollows out a cave on either side of a headland. Eventually the two caves meet and the arch is made.

SAND DUNES

Points: 15

These hills of sand build up behind sandy beaches where dry sand is blown and trapped by plants such as marram grass. Dunes form a natural land defence from the sea.

Points: 20
double with answer

SHINGLE BAR

When waves approach the coast at an angle, sand and shingle are washed along the shore; this is called longshore drift.

What do we use to prevent the effects of long-shore drift?

Points: 20

FOLDED ROCKS

Here you can clearly see how the layers of rocks, from which the land is made, have been folded by forces within the earth's crust.

SCHIST

Points: 20

Look at this rock exposed in a sea cliff. It seems to glisten in the sunlight. It is a mineral called mica that gives this layered rock its shine.

Points: 15

MARRAM GRASS

You will find this tough grass doing a great job by the sea – it builds sand dunes and protects our coasts from erosion.

STACK

Points: 20

A stack is formed from an arch, after the continuous erosion by the sea eventually causes it to collapse leaving the seaward pillar of the arch isolated.

 Points: 25

RAISED BEACH

If you look towards the top of some beaches, you will see that it is made of a shingly or sandy material. This was once the beach and now the sea level has fallen in relation to the land.

WORM CAST

Points: 15

The coils of compacted mud or sand are made by worms living beneath, which pass them out as they extract food from beach material.

Points: 20

STARFISH

Among the creatures that you can find at the shore, a starfish is one of the most exciting. If a starfish loses one of its arms, it can simply grow another one.

BLADDER WRACK

Points: 10
double with answer

Bladder wrack is actually a type of algae. Wrack is a general name given to certain kinds of brown seaweed.

Do you know why it is called bladder wrack?

 Points: 20

FAULT

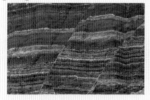

Rocks do not always fold when pulled or pushed by the earth's forces. When they break a fault is created, and the rock on either side can move by different amounts.

COMMON SEAL

Points: 15

From a distance, they look like dogs in the water and are most easily seen on the east coast.

Points: 30   Top Spot!

GREY SEAL

They are inquisitive creatures and will swim with divers given the chance. Grey seals are much larger than the common seal.

Points: 15

Heaths and forests can become very dry in summer so there is always a risk of fire. Workers cut wide channels through vulnerable land to prevent fire spreading and often use them as tracks.

Points: 15

U-SHAPED VALLEY

These valleys were carved into a smooth U-shape by glaciers. You will also see large boulders left by the retreating ice.

Points: 10

MOUNTAINS

Mountains are higher than hills, usually more rugged and rocky and notably higher than the land around. The higher the land, the less vegetation grows.

HEATHLAND

Points: 15

Heath and moorland are types of countryside where the majority of plants grow on acid soils.

CAIRN

Points: 15

Cairns are piles of small flat stones placed on mountain paths. They help travellers stay on the right path and show them the way.

Points: 15

GRANITE

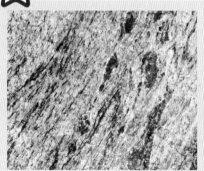

Granite is an igneous rock, formed by cooling magma. It is usually pink, grey or white in colour with large, visible grains. Tors are hills made of granite which have been exposed by erosion of their surrounding rock and soil.

ROCHE MOUTONNÉE

Points: 25

Pronounced 'rosh moo-tonn-ay', this is a rock which has been smoothed and rounded by a glacier passing over it.

Points: 10

MOUNTAIN STREAM

When rivers are close to their source in steeply graded land, they tumble through deep, V-shaped valleys.

LIMESTONE PAVEMENT

Limestone is a rock that can be dissolved by acid. Rainwater is slightly acidic and where the rock is exposed, the rainwater opens up the natural joints in the rock by dissolving it away.

Points: 15

DRYSTONE WALLING

In some areas, such as the Yorkshire Dales, limestone rocks are used to make walls without mortar to hold them together. The bare hillsides seem to have a 'net' of walls dividing them up into curiously shaped fields. To make these walls is a special skill.

HEATHER

Points: 10

With its mauve flowers, heather is a low-growing shrub that grows on heath and moorland. It is often managed by controlled burning to clear the land.

Points: 15

COTTON GRASS

During May and June, the seed heads of this sedge are covered in a fluffy mass of cotton which is carried on the wind.

47

WATERFALL

Points: 15
double with answer

A waterfall forms where there is softer rock downstream from harder rock.

Which is the world's highest waterfall?

Points: 15

MEANDER

In a flat valley floor where the gradient is shallow, a river will flow by swinging from side to side in a series of curves called meanders. This has formed over thousands of years.

BULRUSH

Points: 15

The bulrush can easily be recognised by its female flower which looks like a brown sausage right at the top of a 200cm (79 inch) stalk.

Points: 15

COMMON REED

Millions of starlings use it as a winter roost. During the breeding season countless other birds either nest in it or use its leaves and stems to construct their nests.

COMMON FROG

Points: 15

The frog has a smooth skin and varies in colour from green to yellow. It will live anywhere that is damp but it lays its eggs in ponds.

Points: 15
double with answer

COMMON TOAD

Like frogs, toads also breed in ponds. They are larger than frogs with shorter hind legs and a warty skin.

To what group of animals do frogs and toads belong?

SMOOTH NEWT

Points: 20

Newts emerge from hibernation and head to freshwater to breed. Newts are carnivorous (meat eaters) throughout their life.

Points: 30   Top Spot!

OTTER

The otter is largely nocturnal and secretive due to past persecution. A wildlife sanctuary is the best place to see one.

MINK

Points: 20

Originally introduced into Britain to be bred for its fur, the mink has been released by activists into the wild and is now a major predator of birds, fish and other aquatic life.

FOX

Points: 20

Foxes are surprisingly common mammals and they now find their way into towns and gardens and will even raid dustbins for food, especially at night.

 Points: 35   **Top Spot!**

BADGER

Sadly, you are most likely to see a dead badger killed on the road. But, if you find a sett, you might be able to see one emerge from its entrance at dusk if you stay very still and upwind of the animal.

MOLE

Points: 15
for a molehill, double
with answer

A mole spends almost all of its life underground. You will be very lucky to see a live one above ground, but you can easily find evidence of them from the molehills they leave behind.

What do moles usually eat?

Points: 15

BROWN RAT

An intelligent animal but a serious pest and health hazard. Rats destroy millions of tonnes of food around the world every year and can be found almost anywhere.

WOOD MOUSE

Points: 10

This is probably the creature that you can hear scrabbling about in the corner of a bike shed or even in your attic.

Points: 20

SHORT-TAILED VOLE

This is one of Europe's most common mammals. It moves about using shallow tunnels in grasslands. Their population fluctuates in a four-year cycle.

GREY SQUIRREL

Points: 10

An engaging pest – they strip the bark of young trees, eat the young and eggs of songbirds and carry the squirrel pox virus to our native red squirrel.

Points: 30   **Top Spot!**

RED SQUIRREL

Once common across the whole of the country, this clever rodent is now very rare in England. You can still see them fairly frequently in Scotland, but numbers are declining there too.

Points: 25

This small deer was released into the wild in 1921 and since then it has spread throughout the British Isles.

FALLOW DEER

Points: 20

If you see a deer, it is most likely to be a Fallow Deer. One of our native deer, it has been around for 400,000 years but was almost hunted to extinction in the 14th century.

Points: 20

HEDGEHOG

Hedgehogs are active mainly at night and you can sometimes hear them snuffling around a garden. They are good swimmers and surprisingly agile climbers. Their spikes are there for protection.

BROWN HARE

Points: 20

At first glance a hare looks a little like a rabbit, but it's actually bigger with longer ears and legs. In spring, pairs or even groups can sometimes be seen boxing with one another.

Points: 5

RABBIT

You'll find rabbits in most of the countryside where there is plant food for them to eat and suitable places for them to make their burrows.

Points: 10

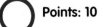

DRAGONFLY

Dragonflies are identified by two pairs of transparent wings and an elongated body. They are normally found around lakes, ponds and streams.

DAMSELFLY

Points: 15

Similar to the dragonfly, you can tell them apart as the wings of most damselflies are positioned parallel to the body when at rest. They are usually smaller and poorer fliers than dragonflies.

Points: 10

HOVERFLY

Although hoverflies resemble wasps, they do not sting. They do however eat huge numbers of aphids and are of great benefit to farmers and gardeners.

LADYBIRD

Points: 5

Everyone likes this colourful insect. There are more than 40 species, they all have spots and some can give you a small bite if annoyed!

Points: 10

BUMBLE BEE

To hear the buzzing of this large, gentle but ungainly bee is to hear the sound of summer.

COMMON WASP

Points: 5

The common wasp can be annoying on picnics, but is useful for the gardener as it feeds on aphids and other garden pests.

Points: 20

A most impressive insect at over 40mm long plus the horns! Its larvae live in rotting tree stumps. In summer they emerge as adult beetles.

Points: 5

The house spider won't harm you, so don't be frightened. Leave it alone in a corner of your room and it will help to keep your house free of flies and bugs all summer long.

Points: 10

This tiny spider has been revered as a good luck charm since Roman times. They can travel great distances by spinning a silk parachute and floating on the wind.

SANDHOPPER

It lives under rotting seaweed or deep in sand. When disturbed it will jump several centimetres to escape.

Points: 15

RED ADMIRAL

This large, brightly coloured butterfly is usually first seen in May or June but, although it is a Mediterranean insect, some individuals do manage to survive the harsh British winter.

PEACOCK

Points: 20

This large, brightly coloured insect may be seen during April and May and then again in September and October.

Points: 15

COMMA

The comma has tattered looking wings for camouflage but it is the pale comma-shaped markings on the underwings which give this butterfly its name.

Points: 20

EMPEROR

The emperor moth is common over much of Britain. You are most likely to find one on moorland and in open country.

BROWN HOUSE

Points: 10

One of two common species of moth found in our homes, the other being the slightly smaller white shouldered house moth. Their caterpillars feed on crumbs and other bits of food that collect around our houses.

Points: 25

LARGE ELEPHANT HAWK MOTH

This very beautiful moth is fairly common and may be found from May onwards, quite often in gardens. The small elephant hawk moth is similar but with less pink on the wings.

INDEX

Answers: P5 Rainbow: Violet, Indigo, Blue, Green, Yellow, Orange, Red. **P8** Daubenton's Bat: False. **P36** Shingle Bar: Groynes. **P40** Bladder Wrack: Because of the air bladders which make its fronds (leaves) float. **P48** Waterfall: Angel Falls in Venezuela 979m (3,212ft). **P50** Toad: Amphibians. **P52** Mole: Worms

i-SPY

How to get your i-SPY certificate and badge

Let us know when you've become a super-spotter with 1000 points and we'll send you a special certificate and badge!

HERE'S WHAT TO DO!

- Ask an adult to check your score.

- Visit www.collins.co.uk/i-SPY to apply for your certificate. If you are under the age of 13 you will need a parent or guardian to do this.

- We'll send your certificate via email and you'll receive a brilliant badge through the post!